W9-DJQ-253

STORM

BRIAN KNAPP

STECK-VAUGHN
LIBRARY

Austin, Texas

First published in the United States in 1990 by Steck-Vaughn Co., Austin, Texas, a subsidiary of National Education Corporation

First published in 1990
by Macmillan Children's Books
A division of Macmillan Publishers Ltd

Designed and produced by Earthscape Editions, Sonning Common, Oxon, England

Cover design by Julian Holland

Illustrations by
Duncan McCrae and Tim Smith

Printed and bound in the United States.

1 2 3 4 5 6 7 8 9 0 LB 94 93 92 91 90

Library of Congress Cataloging-in-Publication Data

Knapp, Brian J.
    Storm/Brian Knapp.
       p.   cm. — (World disasters)
    Includes index.
    Summary: Discusses the generation, types, and benefits of storms and their effects on people.
    ISBN 0-8114-2372-7
    1. Storms—Juvenile literature.   [1. Storms.]
    I. Title.
II. Series: World disasters (Austin, Tex.)
QC941.3.K53   1990
363.3'492—dc20
                                               89-11536
                                                   CIP
                                                    AC

Photographic credits

t = top b = bottom l = left r = right

All photographs are from the Earthscape Editions photographic library except for the following: title page Frank Lane Picture Agency; 34b, 35, AOIS; 16l, 16r European Space Agency; 17 Associated Press; 21; Colorific, 5t Dundee University; 4, 14 NASA; 41b Panos Pictures; 31b, 34t, 40, 42tl, 42br, 43t; 43b; OX- FAM; 12 Popperfoto; 39 Thames Water; 32, 33 UNICEF; 26br, 27br USGS;19 ZEFA

Cover: Nelson Medina/Science Photo Library
Lightning over Tampa Bay, Florida.

Note to the reader
In this book there are some words in the text that are printed in **bold** type. This shows that the word is listed in the glossary on page 46. The glossary gives a brief explanation of words that may be new to you.

Contents

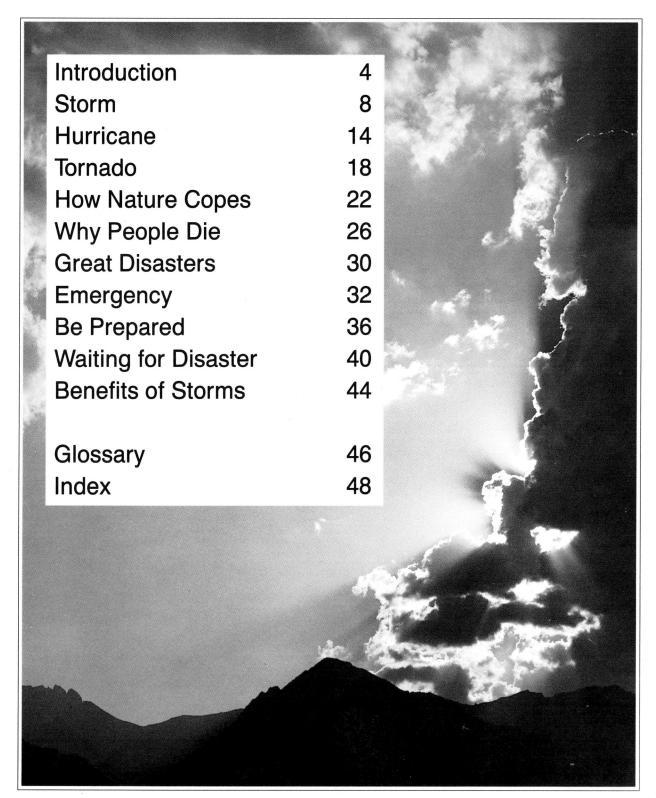

Introduction

The **atmosphere** is one of the most important parts of our world. It provides the air we breathe, and brings rain for the plants which supply our food. Yet it is sometimes a force to be feared. As the air moves across the globe it can form tight spirals. When this happens the wind builds in strength, waves are drawn up to great heights, and a **storm** begins. A storm is a period of very bad weather, and it can cause **disaster.**

There are three major types of storms and they can cause disaster. Storms are a vital part of the natural world, however, and the best people can do is to learn to live with them.

Type of storms

Although storms come in many forms, they are all in some way connected to the growth of huge clouds and strong winds in the atmosphere. A photograph of Earth from space shows where trouble lurks. In some places the cloud appears to curl up tightly into spiral shapes. It is these spiral shaped clouds that produce the most severe storms.

There are three types of bad weather—**depressions, hurricanes,** and **tornadoes**. Depressions bring **gales** to people living outside the **tropics** during the autumn and winter seasons. They cover large areas with driving rain or snow and the winds often cause considerable damage. People may be killed by falling trees and buildings, but most deaths occur at sea when ships sink. In cold areas the storms bring **blizzards.** Sometimes people are trapped by blizzards and die of the cold. Hurricanes are intense and very powerful tropical storms. They often cause many deaths and destroy a great deal of property, but they cover a smaller area than a depression does. Tornadoes are violent whirlwinds that hang down from thunderclouds in long narrow tubes. They can occur in both the tropics and the mid-latitudes, and nearly always leave a trail of complete devastation, even though they are not very big.

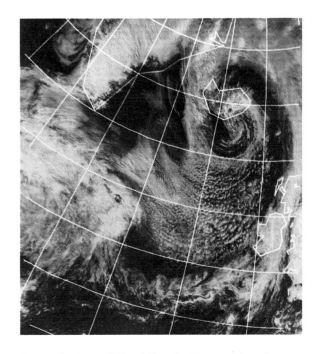

▲ *A view of the Atlantic Ocean showing a depression. The white areas are clouds and the island near the top of the picture is Iceland. The clouds make a pin wheel pattern as they swirl about the center of the depression.*

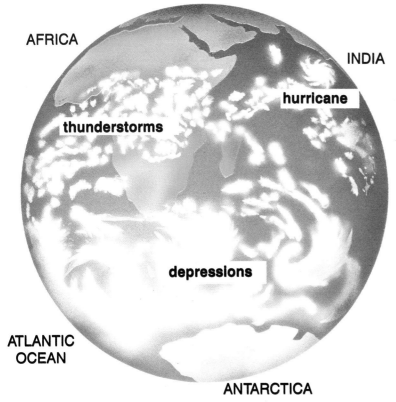

AFRICA

INDIA

hurricane

thunderstorms

depressions

ATLANTIC OCEAN

ANTARCTICA

◄ *A view of the world from space shows the different patterns of storm clouds. Use the sketch to interpret the photograph on the far left.*

Over Africa the mottled appearance of the clouds is made by hundreds of thunderstorms. Above the southern Atlantic the long spiral-shaped clouds form depressions. Off the coast of India there is a hurricane.

◄ *Storms intensify and their winds strengthen as the air spiral tightens. Skaters achieve the same effect as shown here.*

How the atmosphere works

Storm winds are a very special part of the general movement of air across the surface of the Earth. To understand why they form you must know something about how the atmosphere works.

The atmosphere is a huge blanket of gases covering the Earth. It has many layers, but the weather only forms in the lowest layer. This layer, the **troposphere,** is up to 25 miles thick and in it all the clouds form. Above it is the **stratosphere**, a layer of air that acts like a lid, keeping all the weather firmly near the ground.

Air in the troposphere is constantly churning over, driven by the heat from the sun. It shines down most fiercely on the tropics, where the land gets very hot. In turn the land heats the air, creating huge thunderstorms that act like the pistons of the atmosphere, pumping energy into the air all the time.

The sun shines only weakly near the poles. They receive much less heat, and the land and the air are very cold.

The contrast between the hot air at the tropics and the cold air near the poles causes air currents to develop in the atmosphere in a pattern similar to water when heated in a saucepan. The warm air carried aloft by the thunderstorms in the tropics is taken to the poles where it helps prevent these regions from being even colder. Once it has cooled, the air sinks and flows back to the tropics much closer to the ground. Eventually it is warmed and ready to be carried aloft once more.

▲ *The circulation in a saucepan occurs because the water is heated from below. As warm water rises, cooler water sinks to take its place.*

▶ *This map shows the places in the world where severe storms may be expected.*

The reason for storms

The flow of air across the Earth is never smooth for two reasons. In the first place, the Earth is spinning. The spin of the Earth throws the air into curving paths. Then, the pattern of land and sea, mountain and plain causes the air to dip and rise, slow and speed up, changing the way the air flows even more. The twisting and weaving paths that it takes are called **turbulence.** The paths of turbulent air are unpredictable, which is why the weather forecaster's job is so difficult.

In some places curving air paths change and form a spiral of air. All these spirals of air contain enormous amounts of energy. Although the pinwheel shapes made by clouds formed in spirals look beautiful from space, they may spell disaster to people on the ground.

In general the tighter the spiral of air that forms, the faster the air flows and the stronger the winds blow. In many ways this can be likened to the way ballet dancers and ice skaters produce their fast and slow spiraling movements. Dancers can increase their rate of spin by standing up and bringing their arms in. Alternatively, they can open their arms and crouch if they need to slow down. A depression is similar to the dancer with arms wide; its winds are the least fierce, but it affects the greatest area. A hurricane can be compared to the dancer standing up straight: the winds are faster than a depression but occupy less than a quarter of the area. Tornadoes are like dancers tucking their arms in and spinning as fast as they can; the winds are very fierce but are confined to a small ground area, usually no more than a mile across.

When the winds blow fiercely enough, a storm is born.

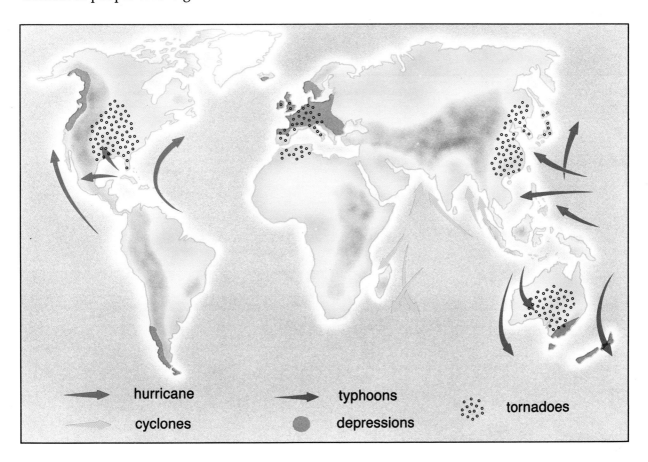

hurricane

cyclones

typhoons

depressions

tornadoes

Storm

When the wind howls and the rain pours down, a storm can be exciting from the safety of home. However, such a storm is rarely a big one. A big storm turns excitement into fear and home may not be a safe place any longer.

The reason for depressions

In the cool **mid-latitudes** spirals of air grow, mature, and decay all the time. These are depressions. They are steered in their wavy paths by fast moving winds high in the air called jet streams.

Depressions are formed at the battleground between cold air returning from the arctic and warm air pushing its way out from the tropics. One well known place where this happens is off the eastern seaboard of North America where moist warm air from the Gulf of Mexico meets cold dry air that has come from Canada. The two types of air push against one another, and eventually the warm air slips around and over the cold air.

Depressions are regions of warm and cold air that have become locked together and are starting to spiral. Eventually the warm air will spiral up and over the cold. Before this happens the strength of the depression will depend on how great the difference in temperature is between the two bodies of air. If the temperature contrast becomes very big, the depression will spiral tighter and tighter, and then a storm will develop.

Fortunately very severe storms that cause disaster are rare. The story that follows is about a storm that hit southern England in the autumn of 1987. This storm did not cost many lives, but it caused a large amount of damage. It was a disaster because people in England were unprepared for such a storm.

▼ *This diagram shows the normal path of the air waves that carry depressions with them. They are known as Rossby waves after the person who first identified them.*

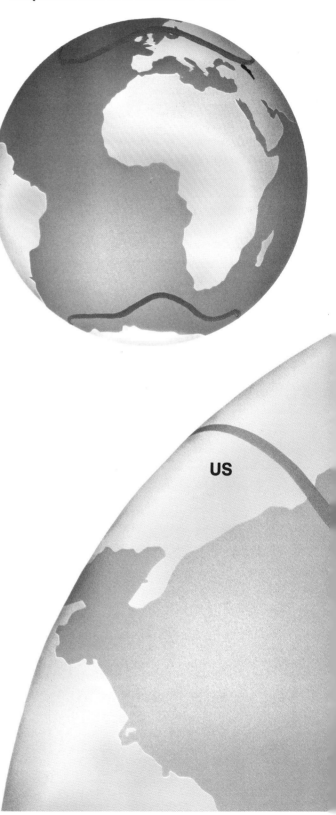

US

The start of the storm

Severe storms are uncommon in Europe. People read about hurricanes in the United States and the fearful damage they cause, but don't believe it could happen in Europe. Autumn 1987 brought the Europeans a big surprise. A freak of weather suddenly brought cold and warm air together and caused a small depression to get deeper and its winds to build. This was no depression on the wane, it was a strengthening giant, about to explode. It would cut a swath of destruction across Europe, the likes of which happens only once every two hundred years.

The Spanish and the Portuguese were the first to suffer. On Wednesday and Thursday they were battered by gales and flooded by torrential rain. But it was northern France and southern England that were to take the brunt of the near-hurricane force winds.

▼   *This diagram shows the path of the center of the storm that brought havoc to Europe in 1987. Notice that it followed a wave-like path from the United States, showing clearly how weather in one part of the world is connected to events elsewhere.*

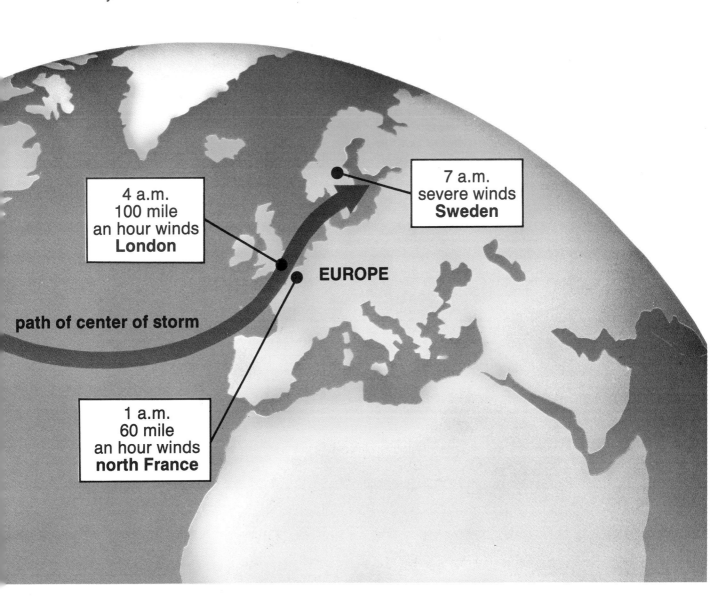

4 a.m.
100 mile
an hour winds
London

7 a.m.
severe winds
Sweden

EUROPE

path of center of storm

1 a.m.
60 mile
an hour winds
north France

The storm hits London

In London that night people went to bed completely unaware of the coming disaster because the forecasters hadn't expected the storm to develop so intensely.

By midnight most people were up and very much awake. The wind was howling with a noise like an express train through the deserted streets. Trees flailed violently back and forth, scaffolding around buildings was torn away, and tiles sucked off roof tops.

▶ *As the storm abated, the people of Folkestone were able to walk along the beach and see the English channel ferry, Hengist, stuck fast on their beach. Storm waves were still beating against her sides even at low tide.*

▼ *The storm left many houses damaged and people quickly had to patch up their roofs with plastic sheets. The people in these houses were lucky; if the wind had blown in a different direction, the trees could have fallen into the houses and wrecked the front rooms.*

Soon the winds grew to near hurricane strength. Many trees simply keeled over, thrashing the nearby buildings with their branches. They crashed into roofs, and fell headlong into the streets, blocking roads. Chimneys toppled and fell, punching great holes in the roofs.

In one of the tall apartment houses about 200 people had to be **evacuated** as a corner apartment had its walls sucked away by the gales, leaving the rest of the building in danger of collapse.

Then the lights went out. Electricity cables coming from distant power stations were flailing wildly in the wind. They slapped together, causing short circuits, then they broke. London's millions were without power.

The storm outside London

What happened in London was happening even more frighteningly all over the south of England and the northwest of France. The storm first hit the northern French coast and the Channel Islands at about 2 a.m. with gusts of up to 135 miles an hour. In the Channel Islands people's livelihoods depend on growing delicate crops in **greenhouses.** Islanders watched helplessly as the glass was smashed by the gusts and the wind ripped at the exposed plants inside. It was heartbreaking.

The gales then hit Hampshire in southern England. Nearly every road in the county was soon blocked with fallen trees,

making it impossible for emergency crews to reach the injured. Two firemen were killed by a falling oak tree that crashed onto their fire engine as they raced to answer an emergency call.

Severe flooding and high winds wracked southwest England but the worst of the wind was felt in Sussex and Kent counties. In the seaside town of Brighton a home for elderly people had its roof ripped right off and thrown to the ground, leaving a number of old people frightened and without shelter in the middle of the night. Nearby mobile homes were tossed about as though they were toys, and dumped upside down and on top of one another. The site soon looked as though a bomb had hit it.

▲ *This view of London's suburbs shows how the wind felled most trees, pushing shallow-rooted species right over. The only tree left standing is a plane tree that had shed its leaves. The felled trees have only missed the houses because of the long gardens.*

In the English Channel and the North Sea, ships ran for cover. More than 800 passengers were stranded on two cross channel ferries, which were unable to dock at the port of Dover. The sea boiled around the vessels in 30-foot-high waves. No one was hurt but they were all shocked by the frightening experience. The ferry *Hengist* had a lucky escape as she was flung against the shore at Folkestone. Then she was left high and dry just yards from the concrete sea wall that could have smashed her side.

At Dover two seamen from Singapore were feared drowned after a ship turned over in the murderous seas. Gales up to 105 miles an hour nearly smashed it into the Dover harbor wall, then flipped it right over.

Both of London's major airports were put out of action when it became too dangerous for planes to land. Thousands of people had to be diverted to other airports long distances away.

Treasured trees in the Botanical Gardens at Kew near London were uprooted. They were part of a collection from all over the world, and it will take 200 years for new trees to grow to replace them.

After the storm

The next morning the gale force winds were still blowing. The police issued warnings asking people to stay indoors. Trains were canceled and railway stations were closed; the London subway could not run because there was no electricity. Few people could get to work and the London streets wore a

◄ *Farmers were among the people to suffer most. Here you see a mature orchard uprooted, every single tree laid on its side. Not only must these trees be removed, but new saplings must be planted. It will take many years before this orchard is providing fruit again. In the meantime the farmer receives no income from the orchard.*

► *After the storm had abated, tens of thousands of people were left with the problem of moving the trees that were blocking their drives. This was not easy to solve because professional help is needed for such large objects. In many cases narrow "cuttings" had to be made through the trunks to allow people to get to and from their homes. More complete removal had to wait for many weeks.*

tattered and deserted look. The forces of nature had brought a great city to a complete standstill.

When the storm finally blew out into the North Sea on Friday afternoon, the toll was 18 people dead and hundreds injured. More than $500 million of property had been damaged, and millions of people left to patch up their houses, repair fences, and pick up their lives as best they could.

The public service crews made heroic efforts, but three days after the disaster many railway lines and roads were still blocked. It was more than ten days before electricity and gas were completely restored. The storm of October 1987 will be remembered in Europe for a long time to come.

Hurricane!

Hurricanes (also called **typhoons** in East Asia and **cyclones** in the Indian Ocean) are tropical storms of great violence, far more powerful than the storms that battered Britain in 1987. In the twentieth century over 45,000 people have been killed by hurricanes in the Atlantic region alone.

Hurricanes begin life near the equator as thunderclouds packed together in a spiral shape. The largest hurricanes spread over hundreds of miles. Big hurricanes may last for many days and even weeks, bringing very severe winds as well as torrential rains to people unlucky enough to be in their paths.

How hurricanes form

At any one moment there may be up to 5,000 active tropical **thunderstorms.** Mostly they stay within the tropics, but occasionally one of them breaks loose, its winds begin to spin, and within a short time great pinwheels of clouds have formed. A hurricane has been born.

Hurricanes are made of strong winds spiraling around an area of calm, called the **eye,** which is just a few miles across. Once formed, wandering hurricanes are like animals—no one can guess what they will

▼ *A hurricane's spiral form is easily seen from space. Notice there are bands of cloud separated by bands of clear sky. The eye of the storm is too small to show.*

do and where they will go next. Once a hurricane has been spotted, it is given a name. A map of hurricanes over the United States shows that hurricanes rarely follow the same path twice.

As hurricanes move they suck in vast amounts of warm moist air just above the sea and carry it upwards. The air loses both its warmth and its moisture as it travels up into the storm clouds. The warmth goes to feed the hurricane and make it stronger, the moisture is released as torrential rain.

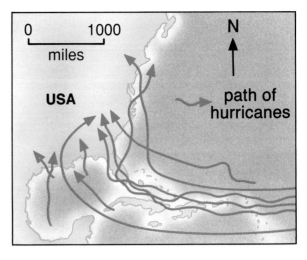

▲ *This map shows common tracks followed by hurricanes off the coast of the United States.*

▼ *This diagram shows a cross section through a hurricane. Air is sucked in at the base, then spiraled toward the top. The giant thunderclouds that make up the arms of the hurricane also produce periods of torrential rain. Between the cloud bands the air is clear and rain does not fall.*

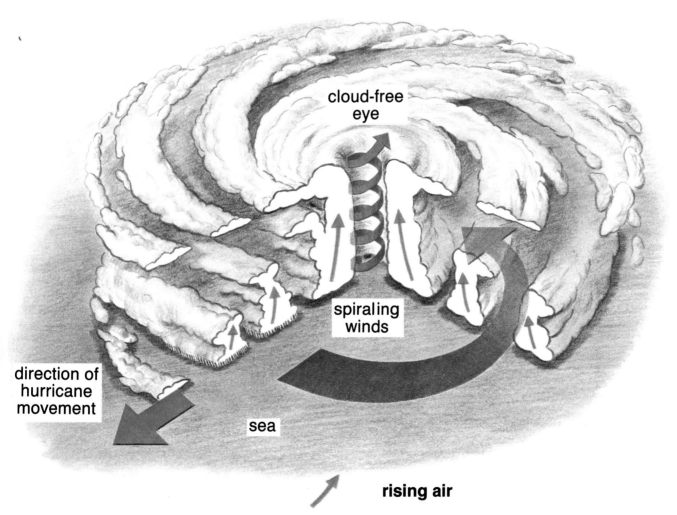

Frederic: Hurricane on the loose

There is a season for hurricanes. In the northern hemisphere it is June to November, in the southern hemisphere it is December to May. At these times weather forecasters keep an especially careful eye on their charts, and study satellite photographs for any tiny sign that a hurricane may be forming. Everything depends on the temperature of the equatorial sea. If it is relatively cool there is a chance that no hurricanes will form. If the sea is warm, however, then it is time to worry.

Some of the most famous hurricanes, like David, Ike, and Frederic, have brought great destruction. Frederic rushed in to the Caribbean Sea in September 1979 to the great dismay of people on the islands there and people who lived along the coast in the southern United States. Many retired people live in wooden houses built along the seashore. They give occupants a good view of the sea, but absolutely no protection from a storm.

So when Frederic was spotted in September 1979 there was great anxiety. As the hurricane crashed through the Caribbean it destroyed the homes of the poor sugar-cane farmers on the island of Dominica. Then it moved in on the city of Mobile, Alabama. When it reached the coast

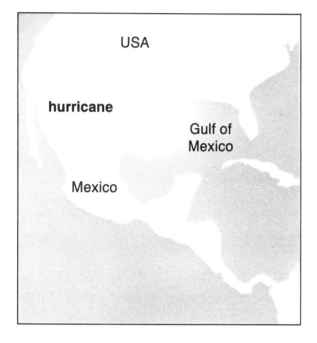

◄ ▼ *These two satellite images show a hurricane moving across the Gulf of Mexico and then crossing the southern coast of the U.S. Some of the world's most famous vacation resorts lie along the Gulf coast and are regularly threatened by hurricanes. The right-hand image shows that hurricanes can sometimes reach well inland, thereby spreading their trail of destruction.*

the storm winds were gusting at 143 miles an hour, sending water surging over the low sand banks at heights of 14 to 16 feet.

The wooden houses stood no chance at all. They disintegrated into matchwood, their contents were flung far and wide, whipped away by the wind. Mobile was soon in ruins. Roofs were ripped off houses, trees were bowled over and laid out flat; windows caved in sending broken glass showering into rooms and onto the street. Where the windows broke the rain streaked in, soaking the contents inside. Within hours $2 billion of damage had been done. Nevertheless, few people were killed. They knew what a hurricane could do, they heeded the warnings and fled inland, leaving nature to do her worst. Had they stayed on the shore to watch the advancing storm, as people did in Galveston in 1900, thousands would have been killed. In that year, 3,000 lives were lost in Galveston by storm waves that reached 23 feet.

Island of no escape

The people of the southern states have somewhere to flee to. The islanders of Haiti, Cuba, the Dominican Republic, Jamaica, and the other islands have no place to go. They just have to sit out the storm in the Caribbean. In 1963 Hurricane Flora killed 5,000 on Haiti when mountain streams, swollen by the torrential rains, burst their banks and flooded through villages. People were washed down the rivers and out to sea where some were eaten by sharks.

Tornado!

Tornadoes, **whirlwinds,** and **waterspouts** are often called **twisters.** Twisters are the short sharp shocks of nature; they last only a few minutes and cross only a few miles before fading away. However, in this time winds can blow at up to 300 miles an hour to make very frightening columns of swirling air. They are the strongest winds found anywhere in the world.

Twisters are usually small—just a few miles across, but very powerful. Tornadoes and whirlwinds occur on land; waterspouts are the same thing as tornadoes and whirlwinds, but waterspouts occur over water.

Tornadoes come in all shapes and sizes; some are long thin rope-like shapes, while others may spread out and look like an upside down bell. However, they all have one thing in common; they can suck big objects from the ground. Waterspouts have even sucked up sizeable ships from the sea!

▼ *This diagram of a tornado shows how air corkscrews up into the base of a large thundercloud. The thundercloud is steered by high-level winds and this, in turn, determines the path that the tornado will follow. To balance the spiraling updrafts that make the tornado, there is a flow of air downward at the rear. This air does not, however, give rise to violent winds.*

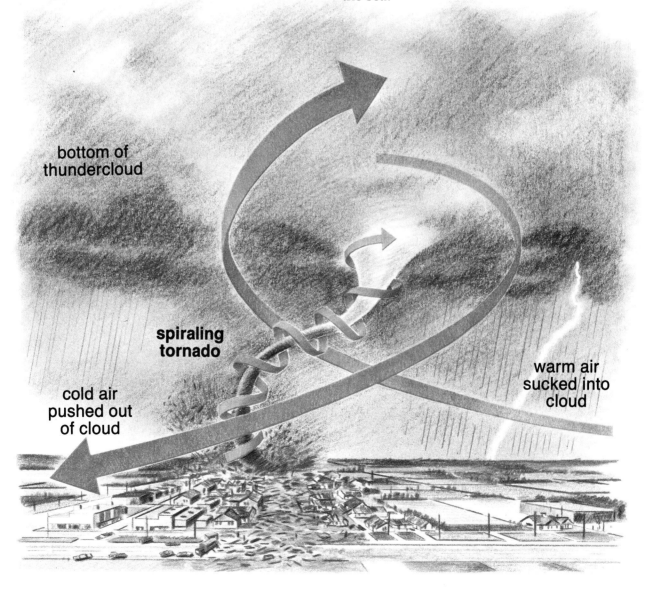

bottom of
thundercloud

spiraling
tornado

cold air
pushed out
of cloud

warm air
sucked into
cloud

The cause of twisters

Twisters form where warm moist air from the tropics meets cold dry air from the poles. This happens along a region in the sky called a front. The big difference in temperature makes the air swirl, and often it rolls up into the column of air we call a twister. It's like an **eddy** found in the fast moving waters of a river. You can't say exactly where or when twisters are going to occur, but you *can* say what kind of weather makes them more likely. Twisters turn up during cloudy weather when there are severe thunderstorms.

What happens in a twister

As a twister approaches, you will see a dark funnel-shaped cloud hanging from the sky, looking something like an elephant's trunk. And, just like an elephant's trunk, a twister sucks up nearly everything it passes over. Up go trees, fences, cars, soil from the fields, and sometimes whole houses to be smashed in the wind's deadly grasp.

You can almost tell what is in a tornado by its color. If the bottom is yellow or brown it is probably holding a mass of soil in the air. If it is a gray color, the chances are that the tornado has ripped up

◄ *You can see the long curving funnel of a tornado clearly in this photograph from Nebraska. The funnel is widest where it leaves the gray base of the thundercloud. The tornado whirls up the soil from the fields causing the brown colored dust storm.*

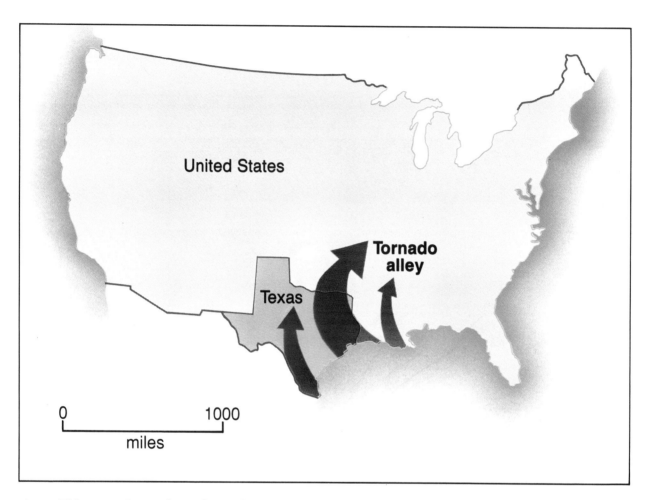

trees, fences, and cars as it smashed its way through a town. A waterspout is more of a light blue in color, because it always contains sea water.

A twister has its own sound effects. In the distance it may appear to make no sound at all, but the arrival of a twister has been compared to the sound of a swarm of bees, followed by the noise of an express train as it gets closer and closer.

As twisters suck air from the ground they lower the air pressure, because air is sucked up in the funnel faster than it can flow in. Because the air pressure is lower on the body, blood expands and people who have experienced a twister say it makes them feel as if their heads are about to explode.

When twisters strike

Usually 850 tornadoes a year strike the United States—more than any other country. Nearly all occur in the early afternoon when the air is at its hottest, and most of these are between April and October, the hottest months of the year.

In some places tornadoes, and their watery cousins, waterspouts, are frighteningly common. Texas and other southern states are visited by hundreds of twisters a year. Because they are so common in this area, the midwestern and south central United States has been nicknamed "tornado alley."

The greatest dangers from a twister occur if you are sucked up into its maw. If you are outdoors when a twister strikes and manage to hold onto something that is not sucked away, you will still be in real danger from flying objects such as pieces of wood

◄　*When a tornado struck Wichita Falls, Texas, it left so much devastation the town almost looked as though it had been blown apart by an enormous bomb.*

and glass. These objects can be hurled through the air with such force that they will penetrate a brick wall.

Sometimes tornadoes smash their way through towns and villages, wreaking great havoc. In Wichita Falls, Texas, a tornado struck on April 10, 1979. It carved a swath of destruction across the city that left 20,000 people homeless, 46 dead, and many more buried in the ruins of their homes.

Occasionally tornadoes can break out by the hundreds. In 1974, 148 tornadoes occurred in 2 days, stretching over 13 states, killing 315 people. The most deadly tornado known occurred in the midwestern states in 1925. It killed 689 people.

Some strange things happen during the fierce winds of a tornado. The wind can shoot a wheat stalk right through a wooden telephone pole just as though it were a bullet. One garage owner had the roof torn off his garage and 200 tires were sucked out, never to be seen again. In another tornado, a chicken had all its feathers plucked off, but it survived to walk around afterward despite its ordeal.

How Nature Copes

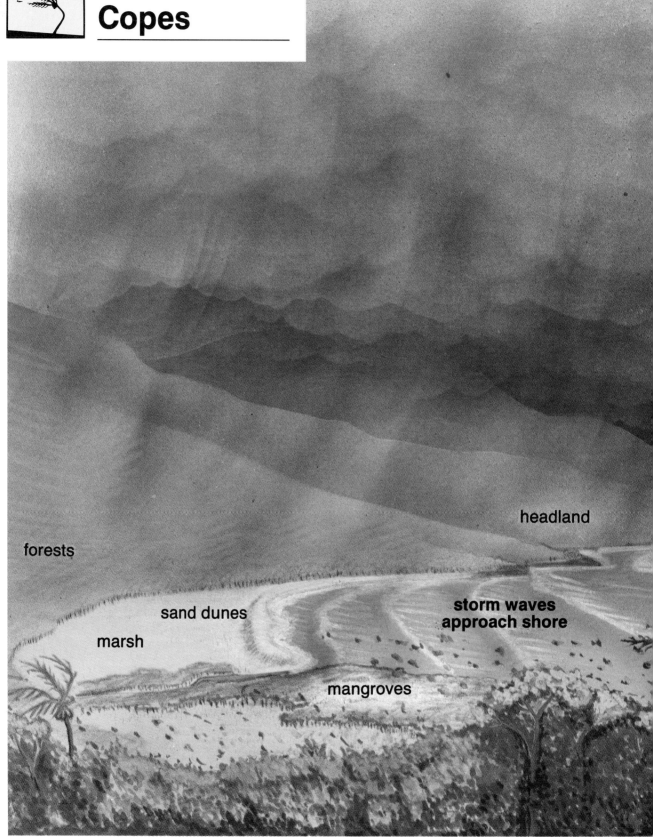

forests

headland

sand dunes

storm waves
approach shore

marsh

mangroves

The amount of energy storms contain makes them almost like natural "bombs" that explode on the landscape from time to time. But what effect do storms have on the natural world? Are severe storms as much of a disaster for nature as they are for people?

The defensive coast

Most natural coasts are protected against storms more effectively than the best fortifications people could build, although at first sight this might not seem to be the case.

Imagine a hurricane bearing down on a coast, its winds whipping up giant towers of waves each capped by white plumes of foam. Can anything stop the hurricane from causing terrible damage? Now look at the coast itself. A whole army of defenses lie in wait!

The first line of defense is the beach. It may only be made of loose sand, but as the storm waves thrash up the beach and hurl sand about, they use up energy. The more energy that is absorbed by the beach, the less there is to damage the land.

The beach alone is usually not enough to break the back of the waves. Next comes the rocky headland where the waves will beat against the cliffs. Some rocks will be broken off, but as they fall into the water these too will help to break the force of the waves.

In the bay there is no rock. Instead there is a forest of **mangrove** trees. They have stilt-like roots that twine in and out of one another then go deep into the sand of a beach or the mud of an estuary. Rising from the roots are thick sturdy trunks that reach about twenty feet from the ground. From the trunks hang branches covered with rubbery dark green leaves that will not easily tear. The mangroves stretch for hundreds of yards inland. When the wind and waves batter the trees, the mangrove forest wall holds firm. Behind the mangroves are wide marshes. The fierce winds carry some water with them right over the mangroves but it is all soaked up in the marsh. The force of the waves has been spent.

◄ *This diagram shows some of the many ways in which natural features absorb the energy of a storm and restrict the damage.*

The storm has been stopped at the coast, but the winds and rain drive on inland. However, there too, defenses lie in wait in the shape of dense forests of a different kind. These forests have many layers with tall, medium, and short trees. Most important, they form a complete and closed leaf layer called a **canopy.** As the rain cascades from the sky in huge powerful drops it hits the canopy and is immediately stopped. All that reaches the ground is the drip, drip, drip from the leaves. Since no rain reaches the soil directly, the soil is not eroded.

In the hurricane force winds, trees flail about and their trunks bend. However, their irregular surfaces act like brakes. They slow down the wind, absorbing the energy of the storm. Some trees may break or be uprooted, but most will stand firm. The wind will only be able to get under the canopy and reach the ground if there are gaps in the forest, and in natural forests such gaps are rare.

▲   *These long mangrove roots are excellent at digging themselves into the beach. The root "spikes" shown here rise from the buried roots and trap sand.*

▶   *The dense rain forest shown here has many layers, each of which can absorb the force of raindrops and lessen the impact of rain on the soil.*

After the storm

In the end the storm passes and the damage to the land has been limited. Nature uses few brick walls and almost no smooth surfaces for her defense. Nothing is placed in even rows, so the wind cannot gain speed in a straight path. Instead nature uses rough, tough, and flexible materials that can readily be replaced. Trees that are broken will be replaced by seedlings; sand lost from the beach will be washed back in the course of time.

If people learn from these examples of nature the number of disasters will become smaller.

▶ *The tree that has been knocked down lets sunlight shine onto the forest floor. This will allow other saplings to grow in its place.*

▼ *This coast in Thailand has many natural tree defenses. Palm trees line the coast, but there is also an extensive forest inland which can absorb more of a storm's energy.*

Why People Die

Although storms are not uncommon, their dangers often go unrecognized until it is too late. Then some people are at risk—and that means some may die.

This story of Mr. and Mrs. Collins gives some idea why people put themselves at risk, even knowingly. Mr. and Mrs. Collins live in New York surrounded by tall skyscrapers. They have been saving all their lives for a place in the sun, and they want to get away from the noise and bustle of the city and head down south. The southern states make up the Sunshine Coast, and there companies have built condominiums and houses for the hundreds of thousands who want to retire. Most face the sea, with the beach just a few steps away and a small jetty for a motor boat. To Mr. and Mrs. Collins, it's a dream world. However, they have never lived by the sea and know nothing of its dangers.

▼ ▼ *The bottom left photograph shows the way many people remember their visits to the shore. The black and white photograph shows a coastal resort near Corpus Christi, Texas, a few days after a hurricane had hit it. The poles show where houses once stood.*

▲ *This is the New York landscape that Mr. and Mrs. Collins know well. They have never lived on the coast.*

Ignoring advice

Mr. and Mrs. Collins went to see their dream house in December. They left the cold of New York for warm southern sunshine. It felt good. As they walked along the beach they came to a little gathering. A man on a bicycle was talking to some older people about the hurricanes that come to these coasts. People who had lived by the sea as long as four or five years were arguing. "There has never been a sign of a hurricane since we've been here. You're just scaremongering."

The man came from a weather institute and he had figures to show there was still real danger. "There may not have been a hurricane lately, but it only takes one. You don't get a second chance!"

Mr. and Mrs. Collins left the little group still arguing and went on with their walk. They were glad they had bought their seaside home. They were still looking forward to moving in next March.

What went wrong

Like Mr. and Mrs. Collins, most of the other people who came to live in the south were from the north. They had even read about hurricanes in the newspapers and seen them on TV, but they had no real understanding of them. In any case, they thought such events would not happen to them. They were proved wrong in 1979. Millions of other Americans planning to retire to the Sunshine Coast may also be wrong. It can happen to them, and it probably will. If they are lucky they will be able to escape inland because the National Hurricane Center usually warns of danger in time. If they are unlucky they will lose what they own and maybe not their lives when the next hurricane comes.

◄ ▼ *These pictures show typical coastal developments that can lead to disaster. The hotels in Ocean City, N.J., (black and white photograph) have been built on a ridge of sand facing the open Atlantic Ocean. Behind them are huge mobile home parks that would be flooded by a storm tide. The housing development in southern England (color) is located on the edge of a beach. It is within yards of the coast, but has absolutely no protection against storms.*

At risk in the developing world

Mr. and Mrs. Collins decided to put themselves at risk even though they had been warned. Mr. and Mrs. Sossillo were not so fortunate, because they did not have a choice. Like most people in the southern part of Asia, they are farmers. However, because all the land in their country has been used, they were forced to try to find new land.

The Sossillos joined with other people in the area to cut down the protective coastal mangrove forest and replace it with

◀ *This village has been built next to the sea so that all the precious soil can be used to grow crops. Farmers have also cut down all the trees that once protected the land. A storm could now threaten the villagers and wash away all the soil.*

▼ *Here you see the result of building new paddy fields where once mangrove forests grew. A storm has breached the paddy walls nearest the sea and flooded the fields with salt water. Only the parts of the coast that still have trees have been protected. The pressure to use every last scrap of land has ruined the work of years.*

rice paddy fields. To try to secure more land for the future, they have built walls into the sea. This will trap mud that can eventually be reclaimed as new paddy fields. However, as they reclaim more and more land that was once sea, they put themselves at more and more risk.

The Sossillos moved to the mud flats on the coast because there was nowhere else to go. All the rest of the land in their country had been used up. The only way they could stay alive and produce their own food was to go to the new land by the sea. They knew it was dangerous. They knew that if a cyclone came they might die. However, they had no choice. Better to take the chance of being caught by a cyclone than the certainty of gradually starving.

Mr. and Mrs. Collins probably would rebuild in the same place if a hurricane ever struck, using their insurance money. If Mr. and Mrs. Sossillo are still alive after the cyclone they too will rebuild, with their bare hands in exactly the same dangerous place.

▲ *Although this building is plainly liable to destruction by storm waves, the residents refused to leave it. They built a new set of stairs at the rear instead.*

▼ *The people who built this hotel on the cliff top did not realize that a large storm could cause the cliff to collapse. They have had to abandon it.*

Great Disasters

"Very early in the morning, there began a very great and dreadful storm of wind . . . which continued with a strange and unusual violence . . ."

So wrote a famous British author and traveler, Daniel Defoe, in 1703. He was writing about Britain's last great storm before the one of 1987, when 8,000 people were killed.

At the end Defoe wrote, "The city of London . . . was a strange spectacle . . . as soon as people could put their heads out of the doors . . . everybody expected (to see) destruction . . . yet I question very much if anybody believed the hundredth part of what they saw." In Defoe's time, two centuries ago, the number of deaths was much higher than in a similar storm today, because people lived in much flimsier built houses. Today people in the **developing world** suffer many more deaths than people of industrialized countries. The reason for this is that people in poorer countries cannot afford to protect themselves very well. Many also have to live next to coasts that take the full force of storms, or by rivers that flood easily.

Nearly all of the great disasters are caused by hurricanes and are found in the region of India and Bangladesh. This part of the world not only has more natural disasters than anywhere else, it is also one of the poorest regions so that people there have few means of protecting themselves. Look at the list of the world's great storm disasters. Notice that today the largest number of people killed is in the developing world.

The World's Great Storm Disasters

Date	Place	Numbers Killed
1703	England	8,000
1864	India	70,000
1876	India	200,000
1881	Indonesia	300,000
1882	India	100,000
1900	United States	7,000
1906	Hong Kong	10,000
1928	United States	2,000
1942	India	40,000
1957	United States	390
1960	Bangladesh	14,000
1963	Bangladesh	22,000
1965	Bangladesh	13,000
1965	Bangladesh	25,000
1970	Bangladesh	500,000
1974	Honduras	8,000
1977	India	15,000
1979	United States	15
1985	Bangladesh	200,000
1987	England	18

The strength of storm winds

Hurricanes are winds that reach over 74 miles an hour. Winds of this speed often tear measuring instruments right off their sockets, but it is probable that in a tornado winds of up to 185 miles an hour are reached.

The size of storm wind is often measured by a scale called the Beaufort scale. A hurricane is at the top of the scale—number 12!

▼ *The 1985 Bangladesh cyclone disaster was one of the worst in recorded history. In this photograph you can see people wandering about looking for their lost possessions after the winds dropped.*

It took many months for these people to rebuild their homes, and years before they were able to start farming properly again.

The Beaufort Scale

Number	Description of Wind	Wind Speed miles per hour
0	calm	0–1
1	light air	1–3
2	light breeze	4–7
3	gentle breeze	8–12
4	moderate breeze	13–18
5	fresh breeze	19–24
6	strong breeze	25–31
7	near gale	32–38
8	gale	39–46
9	strong gale	47–54
10	storm	55–63
11	violent storm	64–72
12	hurricane, tornado	73–82
13–17	extreme violence	83–136

Emergency

When a disaster hits a country many people will need help. However, to be effective, those who come to help in an **emergency** must be clear about what to do. They must understand what happens to people during and after a disaster.

To start with there is usually little panic. Out of the chaos a few people naturally take over the role of leaders and help to organize others. These people may be good with their hands for example, or they may have some medical skills.

In general a disaster pulls people together so that they help one another, even if they are complete strangers.

As soon as the storm has died down people go in search of relatives and friends. The first "teams" break up, and new groups form to dig people out of the rubble or find them safe drinking water.

Rescue

When the rescue teams arrive from outside the disaster area, the victims may be exhausted. With help at hand they may just sit back, happy to be told what to do. However, that will only last for a matter of days. Then the communities will want to be left alone again to rebuild their homes and their lives themselves.

▼ *A temporary relief center being established to provide warm food and shelter for people made homeless by a storm.*

◄ *Children being given relief food by boat. In many developing world countries there is simply insufficient transportation to rescue all the people quickly.*

If people are going to help from the outside, they must be ready to act swiftly. The survivors of a disaster need money and help within the first 20-30 days for it to be useful. Even in massive disasters that happen in poor countries, the aid from outside will never be more than a small contribution, perhaps a quarter of all costs. Emergency teams need to know when to arrive and when to leave.

Emergency in the West

There is a big difference between the way we deal with an emergency in the West and the way people have to cope in poorer countries. Governments have money put aside to use in an emergency and police, fire companies, and hospitals all have plans to cope with a disaster that can be brought into action swiftly. Roads will be cleared, shelters set up in community centers and schools, and people cared for in the vital few days after the event. In the West people have insurance policies. A phone call to the insurance company and a check to rebuild a house, or to pay hotel and hospital bills will be on the way.

The right kind of help

In poorer countries governments do not have much cash in reserve for a disaster. They often need to look to the West for extra help. But providing emergency help needs thought.

Suppose a relief team from a Western country goes in to help after a cyclone has just struck. What is the best way to help? Do emergency workers take woolen blankets and old clothes to keep people warm? Should the medicines and packaged foods that have been brought on the plane go straight to the victims?

This is where thought is required. What would these people normally be doing? Are blankets really of any use in a tropical climate? Will Western food upset their stomachs? (When we go abroad foreign food sometimes disagrees with us, so why not the other way around?) Voluntary aid agencies have found potato chips and spaghetti sauce sent as food aid by people from the West to countries in Africa and East Asia. They have even found—unbelievably—diet foods sent to camps of starving people whose crops were destroyed by a storm.

33

What kinds of homes will be best to replace those that have been destroyed? Ones made of brick and concrete? Then how can these people mend their homes in years to come? They won't be able to afford more bricks and cement. Because of this they might expect help to build them again. Their ability to rely on themselves will have been taken away.

Emergency help is vital to save lives and to bring comfort. Most emergency help is needed by the poorer countries. However, care must be taken or a new disaster of a different kind will be produced. When a hurricane struck the Caribbean island of Dominica, much free food poured into the country. However, this tempted the construction workers to join the lines for free food instead of working at rebuilding the devastated dwellings. As a result construction almost stopped and the period taken for recovery from the disaster was made much longer.

▲　*After a storm animals as well as people need to be fed and cared for. The hay brought in by rescue teams is vital because this man will rely on his animals to help him rebuild his farm.*

◄　*Storms cause much havoc to lines of communication. Power cables will almost certainly have been brought down. Without electric power, many people cannot keep warm, or boil water. As a result public utility employees have to be among the first to enter a disaster zone once a storm has passed.*

Maintaining order

Poor people may be tempted to take advantage of storm damage. Many shop windows will be broken and there may be nobody about to protect the property. Most storm disasters are followed by looting, and many governments impose a dusk to dawn curfew to stop this kind of lawlessness. The curfew makes emergency help all the more difficult, because it stops even rescue teams from getting about easily. So part of the emergency plan must be to bring in a sufficiently large number of police or military personnel to cope with the task of protection.

There may be other problems. Disasters bring shortages of many goods

▲ This photograph of the aftermath of a cyclone that hit Darwin in northern Australia gives a good impression of the need for a plan to cope with emergencies. The people who owned this house are left with nothing. Even their car has been smashed by the collapse of the house. What should be done first? Should they be found temporary homes, or should they be left to telephone the insurance company?

and services. Racketeers can prey on desperate people, asking very high prices for even simple foodstuffs. There is little the authorities can do about this exploitation, but it puts an extra urgency on getting life back to normal as quickly as possible.

Be Prepared

Storms happen quite often, so most people in the world will encounter one at some time in their lives. It makes sense to prepare for it to reduce any risks.

Since storms have as much energy as many nuclear bombs, how is it possible to prevent disaster when one strikes? The first step is to look at the way that natural processes work (see p. 22). These are designed to try to use up the force of the wind gradually by absorbing the energy of the waves, or by sheltering the fragile soil from the rain and wind. People should follow these examples.

Protecting the coast

What is the best way to protect the coast? Nature already provides a wide beach backed by a forest or a bank of sand dunes.

► *This stretch of coast is cleverly protected from fierce storm winds which frequently attack it. There is a network of jetties stretching out from the foot of the cliff. These are backed by a sea wall which will prevent erosion of the chalk rock. In a particularly weak area of cliff the protective wall has been built right up to the top. The protection plan has also been designed to allow visitors to get from the cliff top to the beach easily.*

The beach absorbs much of the force of the waves, and the forest or dunes break the rest. Making a beach wider helps to protect the coast, and this is often done. If you look at a beach and see lots of rocks sticking out into the ocean these are the top of walls called jetties. Their job is to trap sand and build a wide beach. Their only drawback is that they are ugly. In the United States and some other countries sand from offshore is pumped onto the beach during calm periods. It gives a nicer beach to look at, but it is very costly.

Sea barriers

There are many houses beside the sea, because people like the view. So, the next step is to try to stop the storm waves from breaking over seaside homes. Nature backs the beach with sand dunes or forest. But no one wants a forest in place of their view of the sea, so engineers have had to find other ways of taking the force of the waves and protecting the land.

Sea walls either on the coast or just offshore are a common means of protection. Sometimes sea walls have big curves near the top that are supposed to turn the wave back onto itself. Others have steps to break up the waves. Another way of doing the same thing is to pile up "dumbells" on the sand. All these methods are very expensive and only those "places" that are near towns usually get any protection.

People who live on low flat coasts have their own special problem—they can be drowned by **storm surges.** Storms can cause the sea to rise 20 feet or more. The only sure answer is to build a long high sea wall, even if it does spoil the view. People in the Netherlands have built thousands of miles of sea walls (which they call **dikes**). Many Dutch people were drowned in 1953 when there was a storm surge in the North Sea and they do not want storms to kill anyone again. In England there is now a huge wall along the Thames River estuary stretching all the way from the sea right up to London. At the edge of London there is a

◀ ▼ *A sea wall has to take a fierce battering and it is often built with a toothed edge to break up the force of the wave. These photographs show the structure of a toothed wall at low tide, and a plain wall withstanding the impact of a storm wave.*

◄ *The fishing village of Staithes in northern England was built in a shelter of a headland. The houses are then sufficiently protected from severe storms by a simple stone wall.*

▼ *This traditional Malaysian house has been built on wooden stilts to protect the occupants from regular flooding caused by storms. Notice the stairs needed to get up to the front door.*

special feature set into the river. It is called a **barrage** and is one of the biggest engineering projects ever built. When a storm and high water are forecast, great curved walls are raised from the sea bed to close off the river until the danger is past.

Some places can't afford to build dikes or barrages. Where this is the case, the way to stay alive is to live in a house on stilts, in two story buildings, or even high-rise apartments. There is no place to escape a storm surge in a bungalow.

The people who live on offshore islands are in more danger than anyone. A storm means rough seas, and if they take to a boat they risk being drowned if the boat should capsize. On the other hand, if they stay they may be drowned by a storm surge. So a low island is not a good place to be in a storm. It is one place where tall buildings with good solid foundations are essential.

Inland shelter

Storms do not stop at the coast. They drive on inland to lash at any buildings that are exposed. One way of getting protection is to find a sheltered place to build. Fishing villages are built in coves, and country

villages nestle in the folds of hills, to escape storm winds. However, large towns and cities cannot hide away like this.

Brick buildings are able to withstand hurricane winds better than wooden ones. Low buildings are better than tall ones (the opposite of at the coast). If all buildings were single story they would take up too much space, so the only answer is to build upwards as strongly as possible.

Most disasters happen when whole roofs are torn off buildings. This weakens the house, making the walls more likely to collapse. Builders normally rely on the weight of the shingles to hold a roof down. In areas liable to gales or hurricane force winds, however, roofs must be strapped down to the houses. Where hurricanes or tornadoes can be expected, it is also vital to have a cellar. If the building starts to be torn apart at least the cellar should be safe.

Trees also help to shelter houses. But they must not be planted in rows or they too will be blown down. They should be planted in clumps or belts. If there are plenty of shelter zones they will keep the wind off the ground. Planting the right sort of trees is also important. They must be trees with roots that dig deeply into the soil. Those with shallow roots will soon be blown down.

Floods

A storm brings rain as well as winds. Rivers quickly swell and often burst their banks. Floods can cause much damage and cost lives. One answer is to hold back the water in **reservoirs** until the danger is past. Another is to build up the riverbanks (called **levees**).

Explaining the danger

Designing buildings that will stand up to the severe weather is one way of helping to save lives and cut repair bills after a disaster. Educating people about the dangers and how to deal with them is another way of saving lives.

The first thing to do is to give plenty of warning of a storm. Government weather stations use satellites and computers to find and track storms. They also try to predict how severe they will be, and all the information is broadcast as soon as it is on hand. However, people have to listen to weather forecasts and take their advice seriously. In the United States alone there are 40 million people living in places where hurricanes occur often. The National Hurricane Center tries to give 12 hours of daylight warning, which should be enough for people to get out of the danger zone.

◄ *Water flows uninterrupted between the steel clad gatehouses that make up the Thames River barrage. The gates lie flat on the riverbed until a storm threatens. Notice the grass covered dike on the far side of the river.*

Waiting for Disaster

In industrialized countries people can try to design their lives and their homes to prevent disaster. However, the people most likely to suffer a big disaster are those in the developing world. In 1985 disaster came to a small coastal island called Urirchar, Bangladesh. Its story may help to show the problems that face a poor country.

The disaster of 1985

Bangladesh lies in southern Asia next to India. It is one of the countries where storm disaster strikes most often. When Bangladesh became an independent country in 1971, its people were full of hope. They called their country Bangladesh because it means "the golden land." But Bangladesh remains one of the world's poorest countries, and many of its people are close to starvation. Some of the people in most danger of this live by the sea.

The island of Urirchar is not really an island but simply a large mudflat by the sea. Nevertheless, it is home to 6,000 poor farmers. They know they can be washed away in a storm, but they have nowhere else to go. If they do not try farming here they will probably starve instead. It is not much of a choice.

In May 1985 a cyclone roared up from the Bay of Bengal. It was to bring death by night to hundreds of thousands of people. The winds lashed out and the sea boiled as the cyclone approached. The great wave of water, between 10 and 20 feet high, moved relentlessly toward the mudflat at 12-13 miles an hour. The people of Urirchar could not escape from their mudflat because the seas were too rough.

When the cyclone broke over the mudflat, the force of the great wall of water was irresistible. It simply washed away more than half the 6,000 people, their screams unheard in the howl of the gale force winds.

A reporter for the London *Times* visited the scene four days later. This is part of his report:

"Wandering around the remains of a bari (group of huts) is a desolating experience. Brilliant blue cushions are scattered in the mud. The carcasses of cattle, swelling to outrageous size in the heat, point their legs like sextants at the sun. Tumbled among the ruins of their homes the bodies of the

▶ **This photograph was taken in 1974 when a cyclone devastated a large part of the Ganges River delta. Since then many more people have settled on the Bangladesh mudflats. The impact of the 1985 cyclone should not have come as a surprise.**

human inhabitants remain grimacing at the sky... A child's body lies alone, his eyes are wide open staring at the mud where his parents dug a living. A patch of chillies is laid out to dry in the sun, drying still, but ownerless.

"As you fly over Urirchar itself the paddy fields look as if they have been cleaned with a squeegee mop. The houses from above are nothing but a forlorn collection of ragged poles, the thatch dumped in flat patches... between three and four thousand are unaccounted for... swept into the Bay of Bengal."

▶ *The map of Bangladesh shows that the Ganges delta lies directly in the path of advancing cyclones. The area that is frequently flooded by storms has been shaded.*

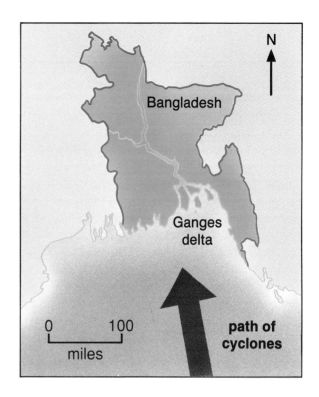

◀ *This man had been surviving in his flooded home for three weeks when the photograph was taken. Nevertheless, because his house remained standing, he must be classed as one of the lucky ones.*

Can the problems be solved?

Bangladesh occupies the place where the mighty Ganges and Brahmaputra rivers finally reach the sea. Together these rivers make up one of the world's largest deltas. This means that Bangladesh is getting bigger all the time, because as the rivers dump their silt in the sea, the huge delta grows and new islands appear almost daily. In years to come the land that is being formed today will be fertile farmland.

There is a problem, however. The number of people in the country is growing so rapidly that there is nothing like enough land. There are new mouths to feed and new farmers looking for land all the time. So the Bangladeshis cannot wait for nature to form the land in her own time. Instead, as each new island begins to surface, people rush to the scene and try to claim a piece of the land to farm for their families.

This is not a good thing to do, because the land they are settling on is still almost at sea level. It is virtually nothing more than a mudflat and will be washed over by high tides. It is not yet ready for crops and the yields will be low for many years. It will, however, yield a little grass for cattle and farmers can also try to grow paddy rice in small fields. So some form of living can be scratched from the land. Most farmers are willing to take a chance.

◀ ▼ The houses shown in the photograph on the left have been built on a part of the Ganges delta where the mud is just high enough to protect the houses from the worst of the floods. The people who built the house below were not as lucky. They were forced to build on low flat land and had to abandon their home as the flood waters rose.

The mudflats are uncomfortable places to live at the best of times. They are also completely open to the sea, and the poor farmers can only make simple huts of bamboo with grass thatch roofs: hardly any protection at all. Worse still, they take their families out onto the mudflats to live where they could all be drowned by the next fierce storm. This is what happened in 1985 to many islands like Urirchar.

Why disaster will happen again

The government has a problem helping these people. It has no other land for the poor farmers, and no money to spend on a sea wall to protect them.

Cyclone disasters are a fact of life in this part of Asia. Weather stations give warnings when a cyclone is on the move, but most people do not own a radio and they never see a newspaper. So how can they be told in time? Even if they *are* told, how can they save themselves when they have nowhere to go? All this spells just as much disaster for the future as it has spelled in the past.

▲   *This is one of the dikes that the Bangladeshi government is trying to build for the protection of its people. These dikes have to be built by hand because there is no money for machines. As a result it is a slow process.*

▼   *The traditional fishermen of the Ganges delta rely on the sea for their livelihood. Without more dikes to protect them, the farmers cannot easily survive and must expect disaster to strike in the future.*

The Benefits of Storms

How can a disaster possibly be of any benefit? People clearing up after a severe storm probably could not think of a single way. But the forces of nature that cause a disaster for some people can actually help the world as a whole.

Severe storms are like short sharp shocks; nature's way of concentrating a lot of energy in one place. The effects can be catastrophic for anyone in their way, but they perform some tasks that cannot be done in more gentle conditions.

▼ *This tropical storm breaking over the Karimoja district of Uganda in Africa was welcomed because it marked the end of the dry season and the start of the growing season.*

Benefits to world fishing

The fish in a fish store's display case are nearly all from the sea. Some fish live and feed on the bottom of the sea, but most fish swim and feed near the surface. They feed on tiny creatures like **plankton**—so small they can only be seen under the microscope. Plankton get their food as chemicals (called **nutrients)** from the muds on the sea bottom. There the remains of dead sea creatures decay and release the vital chemicals on which new life depends.

Normal winds do not stir the sea enough to bring the nutrients toward the surface. But severe storms create such large waves that the whole depth of the sea is disturbed. After a storm the sea often looks murky and unpleasant because there is so much debris suspended in it. But that debris contains the vital nutrients. Without storms there would not be so many nutrients in the water, which would mean fewer plankton, and finally fewer fish for us to eat.

Fighting forest fires

Fires are commonplace in dry, hot parts of the world. Many of them begin through natural causes such as a flash of lightning which may set fire to tinder dry trees or grasses. But forest fires can rage out of control and threaten homes and lives. Often they spread across the landscape on a wide front and firefighting teams simply cannot cope. Even planes dropping "bombs" of water can sometimes do very little. But the torrential rain from a storm falls over large areas. It can douse the flames of the fire and make nearby areas so wet they will not catch fire. Sometimes firemen long for a natural severe storm to stop a fire disaster.

Balancing temperatures

Storms also carry heat from the tropics to the poles helping to even out world temperatures. If this didn't happen the tropics would get hotter and hotter and life there would be impossible. Without heat from the tropics, ice at the poles would stretch much farther. At any one time in the tropics there may be up to 5,000 thunderstorms in action, taking hot air away from the tropics and up to the poles. Hurricanes simply do the vital job of carrying surplus energy quickly across the Earth. In the middle latitudes the

depressions swirl around and push vast amounts of polar air back to the tropics for reheating. They also make a great deal of bad weather for people at the same time.

Relieving drought

Severe storms can bring life back to drought stricken lands. These storms are called the monsoon. In the tropics the "winter" dry season is difficult to dislodge. Dry air sits over continents like Asia and rain-bearing winds cannot get in. People are then in real danger of facing drought. A great concentration of energy is needed to make big clouds that will bring rain. Severe thunderstorms, sometimes hurricanes, do just this job.

Helping natural selection

In most forests there are trees in the fullness of life and those that are starting to die. There are also trees that have become diseased. These old or diseased trees will not have strong branches or roots, and they will be knocked over readily by strong winds. On the other hand the healthy trees will better withstand the full force of a storm. In this way storms help to remove the old and diseased trees providing spaces in the forest where new healthy trees can grow.

Glossary

atmosphere
the thick layer of air that surrounds the Earth. It consists of many layers, or shells, each with different properties.

barrage
a structure built across a river to regulate the flow and help shipping

blizzard
a storm that involves driving snow

canopy
the topmost level of leaves and branches in a forest that protect the ground below from heavy rain

cyclone
an alternative name for a hurricane used in southern Asia

depression
spiraling regions of the atmosphere where warm and cold air are drawn together. Depressions belong to the mid-latitudes and give widespread rain.

developing world
countries that have not yet fully industrialized and which do not have a wide range of health, water, and other facilities open to the majority of the people. In most developing countries the majority of the people work as farmers.

dike
a long earth bank designed to keep water from farmland. The earth bank is usually surfaced with stone to resist erosion.

disaster
a catastrophic event that disrupts the normal lives of people

eddy
a short-lived column of swirling air or liquid produced as part of turbulent movement

emergency
an unforeseen event that requires immediate action to prevent disaster

evacuation
an organized movement of people to get them clear of a danger zone

eye of a hurricane
the central region of a hurricane where there is no cloud and conditions are perfectly calm. It is usually only a few miles across.

gale
a wind speed over 37 miles per hour but less than 74 miles per hour

greenhouse
a place for growing delicate "green" crops under glass. It consists of a thin wooden-framed building with very large areas of glass. This allows the maximum amount of sunlight to reach the plants inside.

groyne
fence of wood or concrete dug into a beach. Groynes are intended to stop sand from being washed away during a storm.

hurricane
a storm containing violent winds over 74 miles per hour

levee
an earth bank by the side of a river which helps to keep river water from flooding across the landscape

mangrove
a tropical tree that lives along the shore and can tolerate salt water. It has stilt-like roots that stand up from the beach and help hold the sand in place.

mid-latitudes
the part of the Earth between the tropics and the arctic zones

nutrients
the chemical foodstuffs that are used by all living things for their growth

plankton
microscopic sea organisms that float in the water. They are the principal food for many fish.

reservoir
an artificial lake contained by a dam. It is used to control the amount of water in a river, to prevent flood or drought, or as a storage area for water.

sea walls
concrete or sheet steel structures that act as a barrier to the waves. They are very expensive to build and are usually found only near heavily populated areas.

storm
severe weather, usually consisting of strong winds and possibly heavy rain or snow

storm surge
an extra high level of water at a coast caused by a storm driving the sea onshore

stratosphere
a layer of air in the atmosphere above the troposphere. It does not contain any clouds and acts to hold the weather in the layer nearest the earth's surface.

thunderstorm
an outburst of heavy rain or hailstones from a single cloud. "Cumulus" clouds produce heavy rain. They are often accompanied by lightning and thunder.

tornado
an extremely violent storm with winds exceeding 74 miles per hour. Tornadoes are associated with a funnel-shaped cloud and very localized damage.

tropics
the Earth's region nearest the equator, containing most of the world's hot lands

troposphere
the lowest layer of the atmosphere. It is the layer that contains all the world's clouds and where all the weather is made. It reaches from the ground to about 10 miles above the Earth's surface.

turbulence
the unpredictable swirling of air as it moves over a spinning Earth

twister
a nickname for a tornado or waterspout

typhoon
an alternative name for a hurricane used in eastern Asia and the Pacific

waterspout
another name for a tornado over water. The funnel that reaches up from the ground to the base of the cloud is composed mainly of water.

whirlwind
another name for a tornado

▼ *A storm over Bombay, India.*

Index

363.3   Knapp, Brian
K
        Storm

$15.95

DATE			
99			